Big Bo Peep

Written and illustrated by Jonathan Allen

Chapter 1

Have you heard the old song called "Little Bo Peep"? It was about a pretty little shepherdess who kept losing her sheep.

Well, I bet you didn't know that Little Bo Peep was a real person and that she had a sister called Big Bo Peep. Big Bo Peep was big and tough, and she never lost her sheep.

When somebody wrote that song about Little Bo Peep, it was a big hit.

Little Bo Peep became famous. I'm sorry to say it made her very big-headed. She went off to be a star, and she left Big Bo Peep to look after the sheep.

Now, deep in the forest there was a Big Bad Wolf. Like most wolves he was very lazy. So, when he heard a song about a shepherdess who kept losing her sheep, his ears pricked up.

"Lost sheep?" he said. "Down at Bo Peep's place? Dear, oh dear. I must go and help. I'm good at finding sheep. In fact I *find* them totally delicious! Ha ha ha!"

That day, Big Bo Peep was mending a stone wall. Suddenly, she heard a noise at the other end of the field. The Big Bad Wolf was trying to steal one of her lambs.

She narrowed her eyes and set off across the field. The wolf saw her coming.

"That must be the silly little shepherdess," he said to himself. "She can't have seen me or she'd have run away by now. I'll give her a growl. That will scare her off."

"Grrrr! Go away, silly little shepherdess!"
growled the wolf.

But Big Bo Peep didn't run off. Instead, she grabbed the wolf by the scruff of the neck.

"Listen, fur face!" she shouted. "Leave my sheep alone. Go on, leave it … OK, I'll just have to tie you in a knot and throw you over that wall!"

Then Big Bo Peep carried on mending her wall.

Chapter 2

Up in the hills there was a band of robbers.
One day they were listening to a song
on their stolen radio. The song was about
a shepherdess who kept losing her sheep.

"Terrible!" said the robber-chief. "Some people shouldn't be allowed to keep sheep! In fact, I think someone should take those poor little sheep away from her."

"You're right!" laughed his band of robbers.

"Let's go and rescue a couple of nice, fat lambs! Ha ha ha!"

That day, Big Bo Peep was fixing the fence. She heard a noise, looked up and saw four men chasing her lambs.

She narrowed her eyes and set off across the field. The robber-chief saw her coming.

"Well, if it isn't Little Bo Peep!" he cried.

"If you want my sheep," said Big Bo Peep slowly, "you can arm-wrestle me for them!"

The robbers stopped laughing and looked at
their chief. He raised his eyebrows.

He liked a girl with spirit.

"All right!" he grinned.

Big Bo Peep smiled back.

The wrestling match didn't last long.
Big Bo Peep beat the robber-chief in no time.

"All right, you win!" he panted.
"But can I ask you a question?"
Big Bo Peep nodded. "What is it?"
"Will you marry me?"
Big Bo Peep paused.

"All right," she said. "But only if you give up robbing and become a sheep farmer."

"All right," said the robber-chief. "It's about time I settled down."

They were married that week. They lived happily ever after and ran the best sheep farm for miles around.

But nobody ever wrote a song about them.